What Is the Civil Rights Movement?

by Sherri L. Smith

illustrated by Tim Foley

Penguin Workshop

In memory of John Lewis and our ancestors for
their strength, dignity, and humanity, and for the
example they set for future generations—SLS

For Walter—TF

PENGUIN WORKSHOP
An Imprint of Penguin Random House LLC, New York

Visit us online at www.penguinrandomhouse.com.

Library of Congress Control Number: 2020033618

ISBN 9781524792305 (paperback)   10 9 8 7 6 5 4 3 2 1
ISBN 9781524792312 (library binding)   10 9 8 7 6 5 4 3 2 1

Contents

What Is the Civil Rights Movement?

One afternoon in March 1955, fifteen-year-old Claudette Colvin boarded a public bus for home. A deep brown-skinned girl with large, dark eyes and black-rimmed glasses, Claudette was a high-school student in Montgomery, Alabama.

On the bus, Claudette and three friends took seats in a row for Black passengers.

At the time, public buses in the South were segregated by race. (Racial segregation meant keeping Black people separated from white people.) In Alabama, white passengers sat in the front rows marked by a sign that read "White." Passengers of color had to take seats in rows behind the sign. If more white people boarded the bus after the "White" area was full,

Black passengers who had seats were forced to give them up.

That's what happened to Claudette and her friends when a young white woman boarded the bus on their trip home. The other girls gave up their seats. But Claudette did not. Just for that, Claudette was arrested! She was locked up in an adult jail cell. "I can still vividly hear the click of those keys," she later said.

What made a teenage girl act so bravely?

At school, Claudette had learned about Harriet Tubman and Sojourner Truth. Both African American women had fought for years against the injustice of slavery.

Harriet Tubman   Sojourner Truth

Claudette believed staying in her seat was doing what they would have wanted her to do. She said, "It felt as though Harriet Tubman's hands were pushing me down on one shoulder and Sojourner Truth's hands were pushing me down on the other shoulder. I felt inspired by these women because my teacher taught us about them in so much detail. I wasn't frightened, but disappointed and angry because I knew I was sitting in the right seat."

Ida B. Wells (1862–1931)

Like Harriet Tubman and Sojourner Truth, Ida B. Wells was an early activist for African American civil rights. An activist is someone who takes action for a cause they believe in. Wells was a Black journalist from the South.

Her best known writing was about the horror of lynching. Lynching is when a mob or group of people commits murder. Many Black people were lynched across the South for false crimes. Wells wrote about these evil killings for audiences around the world. White people where she lived in Memphis, Tennessee, were so angry about her work that they burned down her office and chased her out of town!

But Wells didn't give up. She worked for justice her entire life. In 1909, she helped create the National Association for the Advancement of Colored People. The NAACP helped plan many civil rights protests. It still exists today.

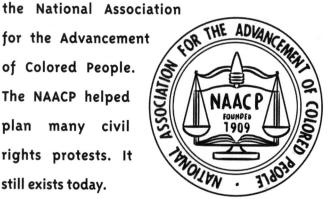

Claudette took a stand for civil rights that day. *Civil rights* are protections promised to all citizens of the United States of America—like the right to vote or the right to an education. Big changes can start with the bravery of a single person. Claudette was one of the many brave people who would work together for the three great promises of America—life, liberty, and happiness.

CHAPTER 1
A Troubled Past

When people talk about the civil rights movement, they usually mean the period in the 1950s and 1960s when African Americans fought for the same rights that white people had. Segregation was the worst in the South. Besides having to sit in separate rows in buses, Black people went to separate schools, drank from separate water fountains, stayed in separate hotels, lived in separate neighborhoods, and were not allowed to vote.

The United States Declaration of Independence says "all men are created equal." But when it was written in 1776, one out of every five people was enslaved. They had been kidnapped from Africa and sold to white Americans like property.

In the Southern states, white people depended on slave labor to run their farms and plantations. But many Northern states wanted to make slavery illegal. Rather than agree to this, in 1860 eleven Southern states began to break away. In 1861, they formed a new country—the Confederate States of America. It included Alabama, Florida,

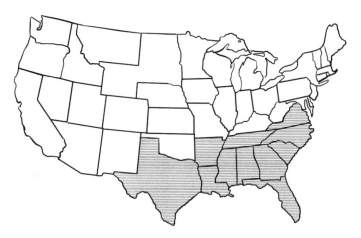

The gray area shows the Confederate states.

Georgia, Louisiana, Mississippi, South Carolina, Texas, Arkansas, North Carolina, Tennessee, and Virginia. The border states of Kentucky and Missouri had divided loyalties. The North wanted the states to stay united. This led to the Civil War.

American Civil War

When it ended in 1865, the South had lost and slavery in the United States was over at last.

The following year saw the first Civil Rights Act. It said all people born in the United States were considered US citizens. As citizens, Black people now had the right "to full and equal benefit of all laws as . . . enjoyed by white citizens." In 1870, a new Civil Rights Act attempted to support Black men's right to vote as granted by the Fifteenth Amendment.

Even so, African Americans continued to face discrimination. Discrimination means they were treated differently because of the color of their skin. The Southern states created new laws that denied African Americans their rights. These were called the Black Codes, also known as Jim Crow laws.

Jim Crow was a character in music shows that made fun of Black people. White actors would darken their faces with burnt cork and dress in rags. Jim Crow was clumsy and not very smart. He was meant to insult Black people. Jim Crow laws were used to make Black people second-class citizens. Second-class citizens are people who are not given equal rights.

Jim Crow laws made it hard for Black citizens to lead a decent life. White people would not sell farmland to Black people or allow them to attend good schools. African Americans were prevented from voting so they could not elect people who would fight on their behalf.

Many African Americans moved to the North or out West for a better life. From 1915 to 1970, around six million Black people migrated from the South. They still faced racism and unfairness. But life was harder for those who remained.

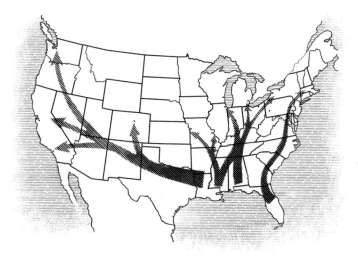

The different routes to Northern states

Racism was not restricted to the South. Even the Supreme Court ignored the rights of Black citizens. The Supreme Court is the highest court in the nation. What it says is the law remains the law.

In 1896, a case went before the Supreme Court. The case was called *Plessy v. Ferguson.* Homer Plessy was a Black activist who challenged a new law in Louisiana that blocked people of color from riding in "white" train cars. This law took away freedoms Plessy had grown up with during Reconstruction. With his fair skin color he was able to buy a ticket for the "white car." But a train conductor threw him out. Plessy and a local civil rights group filed a legal complaint.

Homer Plessy

The Ku Klux Klan

After slavery ended, some white men in the South created a group called the Ku Klux Klan. It's also known as the KKK or "the Klan." Klan members believe in white supremacy. They think white people are superior to Black people. There are about three thousand Klan members in the United States today.

In the past, the Klan often attacked and murdered Black people. Klansmen would wear white robes and pointed white hoods that covered their faces during lynchings. That way no one could tell who had committed the crime.

The Klan attracted members in both the North and South. But not all white people were Klansmen. Some, including Southerners, believed Black people should be treated as equals. But it was not always safe for them to say so. Their lives were at risk.

Everyone lived in fear.

But some brave people began to stand up for themselves. No amount of fear could stop them from fighting for their civil rights.

The Supreme Court judges said Homer Plessy did not have the right to sit in the "white" car. They said segregation was legal as long as both white people and people of color were given "separate but equal" accommodations. (For trains, "accommodations" would mean the seats, and access to food and a bathroom.) While accommodations were indeed kept separate, they were far from equal. Particularly in the South. And yet, for the next sixty years, "separate but equal" was the law of the land.

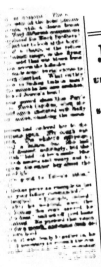

CHAPTER 2
A Long Walk to School

Schools in the South were separate but not equal. White schools were in nicer buildings, with new textbooks and school buses. Black students often walked long distances to school in all kinds of weather. Black schools received old textbooks thrown out by white schools. Some didn't even have flushing toilets!

A white classroom   A Black classroom

It was hard to get a good education if you were Black. That meant it was harder to get a good-paying job.

Seven-year-old Linda Brown had a very long walk to her school in Topeka, Kansas. As she later recalled, "It was several blocks up through railroad yards, and crossing a busy avenue, and standing on the corner, and waiting for the school bus to carry me two miles across town to an all-Black school." In the winter, the walk was unbearable. "I remember walking, tears freezing up on my face, because I began to cry because it was so cold."

Linda Brown

Why couldn't she go to the other school just a few blocks from her house? Because it was for whites only.

In 1951, Linda's father went to court. He said not allowing Linda to go to the local white elementary school went against the Fourteenth Amendment's promise of equal rights. A famous civil rights attorney named Thurgood Marshall brought the case all the way to the Supreme Court. He went on to become the first Black Supreme Court justice.

Thurgood Marshall

On May 17, 1954, the court declared segregation in public schools to be unconstitutional. Unconstitutional meant it went against the laws laid out in the US Constitution. The court said separate could never truly be equal. Schools should start integrating right away. Integration means to mix separate groups together. The decision was called *Brown v. Board of Education.*

But many white people ignored the law.

The city of Little Rock, Arkansas, did not integrate schools until September 1957. The first Black students to do so were known as the Little Rock Nine.

The Little Rock Nine

The local White Citizens' Council was unhappy with the news. The Citizens' Council was like the KKK. But instead of hiding behind robes and hoods, they were businessmen. They used money and friendships with politicians and the police to get their way.

The Citizens' Council threatened the Little Rock Nine as well as their families. Angry white people from all over the South came to town to block the entrance to the all-white Little Rock Central High School.

On September 4, eight of the nine students were driven to the school, only to be stopped by the National Guard. The National Guard is a volunteer US military group. The governor of Arkansas had sent them to stop the teenagers from entering the school. Unfortunately, one student's family did not have a telephone and did not know about the carpool. So Elizabeth Eckford ended up facing the mob all alone.

Elizabeth Eckford on her first day at Central High School

News cameras snapped pictures of the brave girl holding her head up as people spat and yelled at her. But the Guard would not let her inside.

On September 23, all nine students entered the school together using a delivery entrance. But the angry crowd outside stormed the building and the Little Rock Nine were forced to flee.

President Dwight Eisenhower sent 1,200 soldiers and the National Guard back to Central High to keep the peace. On September 25, the Little Rock Nine entered the school with an armed military escort. One of them said, "For the first time in my life, I feel like an American citizen."

Military protection remained in Little Rock for the rest of the school year. Even so, the Little Rock Nine were bullied by white students and teachers alike. One day, Minnijean Brown was tripped in the cafeteria and ended up dumping a bowl of chili on a white boy's head! A few months later, Minnijean was kicked out of school for trading insults with another white student. But the other eight kids remained. Ernest Green was the first Black graduate from Central High. No one clapped when he received his diploma, but he had survived.

The Little Rock Nine had one another. But in New Orleans, Louisiana, one little girl had to face the crowds alone. Her name was Ruby Bridges and she was only six years old. On November 14, 1960, Ruby was taken to an all-white elementary school by US Marshals. Marshals are federal law enforcement officers.

At first Ruby thought the crowd of white people outside of the school was a parade. Then they started shouting threats and throwing eggs at her. White parents dragged their children out of the building. In the end, only one teacher agreed to take Ruby on, but no other students joined her class. Many years later, Ruby said protesters outside the school "didn't see a child. They saw change, and what they thought was being taken from them."

Two years later, an even bigger mob greeted James Meredith at the University of Mississippi in Oxford. (The school is also known as "Ole Miss.") The crowd threw rocks. Guns were fired. A white journalist was killed in the fighting. President John F. Kennedy had to send federal troops onto campus to stop the violence. The troops used tear gas and force until the mob fell apart. It took five hundred US Marshals to protect Meredith as he registered for classes. Soldiers remained with him until he graduated in 1963. Meredith spent the next two years overseas, earning an economics degree in Nigeria. He returned to the United States in 1965 to earn his law degree and continue the fight for civil rights.

James Meredith graduates from the University of Mississippi.

CHAPTER 3
The Montgomery Bus Boycott

If you ask people when the civil rights movement really began, some will say in 1955 in Montgomery, Alabama. On December 1, a woman named Rosa Parks was riding home on a bus. Parks was a seamstress, and she was tired after a long day of work. She also was tired of the racist rules for bus seating. When the driver asked her to give her seat to a white person, she refused.

The bus driver said he would call the police. Parks said, "Go ahead." She was only five feet, three inches tall, but she was determined to stand up to injustice by staying put.

Rosa Parks

Two policemen arrived on the scene. Parks asked one of them, "Why do you push us around?" The white officer replied, "I don't know, but the law is the law and you're under arrest." That arrest led to the yearlong Montgomery Bus Boycott. A boycott is when a group of people refuse to buy or use a certain item or service.

The next day, volunteers sent flyers around the city asking folks to stop riding the public buses for a single day. On Monday, December 5, over 90 percent of all Black riders boycotted. They walked, carpooled, or rode bikes to work and school. Buses moved through the city nearly empty. The protest worked so well, they decided to keep it going. A young minister became the leader of the boycott. His name was Dr. Martin Luther King Jr.

Dr. Martin Luther King Jr.

Under Dr. King, the boycott swelled from one day to a full year. The protesters had three simple goals: (1) to be treated with courtesy by white bus drivers; (2) to have first come, first served seating regardless of skin color; and (3) to have Black bus drivers in Black neighborhoods.

A Black group called the Montgomery Improvement Association bought station wagons to use as taxicabs to help boycotters travel to their jobs. Women raised money to pay for the cars, gas, and insurance by selling food. The bus company was losing money daily. Without buses to bring Black customers downtown, white-owned stores began to lose business.

The Montgomery bus company tried to punish the boycotters by stopping service to Black neighborhoods. Some white people threw firebombs at Dr. King's house. Four local churches were bombed. King and other boycotters were arrested. They were told to pay a $500 fine or spend a year in jail. But the Black community would not give up.

In February 1956, a Black woman named Aurelia Browder joined forces with Claudette Colvin, Mary Louise Smith, and Susie McDonald to file a lawsuit against the mayor of Montgomery. It was dangerous for a Black person to sue a white person. But Browder said, "If you live and you haven't stood for anything, you didn't live for anything, either."

On December 20, 1956, the US Supreme Court declared Montgomery's segregation laws unconstitutional. Browder had won! The Montgomery Bus Boycott was over. It had lasted 381 days and cost the city of Montgomery nearly $1 million. The following morning, the boycott leaders sat in the front row of the first desegregated bus. A major victory had been won for civil rights!

The Club from Nowhere

Georgia Gilmore worked as a cook at a segregated lunch counter. She was determined to do her part to help the Montgomery Bus Boycott. Many people were afraid to openly support the boycott. Their white bosses and landlords might get angry. So Gilmore came up with a plan for women to sell food and give their earnings to the boycott. If anyone asked where the money came from, they'd reply, "Nowhere." And so the women became known as "the Club from Nowhere." They made fried chicken, pork chops, and sweet potato pies to raise money for the cause.

It's possible her involvement cost Gilmore her job. Dr. King encouraged her to open a restaurant. She did so successfully inside her own home. She even cooked for presidents!

Georgia Gilmore

Emmett Till (1941–1955)

"We want to see the boy from Chicago." Those were the words of two white men who showed up in the middle of the night at a house in Mississippi. They were looking for fourteen-year-old Emmett Till. Emmett was a sweet-faced Black kid who loved to tell jokes. In the summer of 1955, Emmett traveled to Mississippi to visit relatives. His mother had not wanted him to go. Chicago had its race problems.

But the South was particularly dangerous for Black boys.

On the night of August 24, Emmett and his cousins went into Bryant's Grocery and Meat Market in Money, Mississippi. The cashier was a white woman named Carolyn Bryant. What happened next is uncertain. Carolyn told her husband and brother-in-law that Emmett had grabbed her and asked her for a date.

A few days later, a group of men lynched Emmett. His body was found three days later by a group of boys out fishing.

Newspapers around the world carried the story and the photo of Emmett's body. The attention shined a spotlight on lynching. But the all-white, all-male jury set his killers free. A few months later, when Rosa Parks refused to give up her seat on that bus in Montgomery, she said, "I thought of Emmett Till and I just couldn't go back."

CHAPTER 4
The Lunch Counter Sit-Ins

The Montgomery Bus Boycott was a nonviolent protest. Many civil rights protesters first learned about nonviolence from Dr. King. He followed the beliefs of an activist in India named Mahatma Gandhi. Gandhi said when violence "appears to do good, the good is only temporary; the evil it does is permanent." On February 1, 1960, another kind of peaceful protest began. It, too, changed the way Black people were treated in America.

Mahatma Gandhi

It started with four friends who were students at an all-Black college in Greensboro, North

Carolina. They stood up for their rights by sitting down. Their local Woolworth store had a "whites only" lunch counter. Joseph McNeil was one of the students who started the protest. He said, "To face this kind of experience and not challenge it meant we were part of the problem."

That Monday afternoon, the four friends each purchased something in the store. Then they took seats at the lunch counter.

"I'm sorry. We don't serve colored here," the white waitress told them.

McNeil and his friends had been inspired by Dr. King's sermons on nonviolent protest. They politely showed the waitress and the diner's manager receipts for what they'd bought. Some white patrons cursed at them. Some encouraged them. The four men feared for their lives, but they held fast. They were not served that day, but they were not arrested, either. They didn't go home until the store closed.

Word of their protest traveled, and the young

men became known as "the Greensboro Four." Their sit-in launched a new era of student involvement in the civil rights movement.

The next day, more students joined the Greensboro Four at Woolworth. The following day, over sixty students filled most of the seats in the diner. By the end of the week, hundreds of Black and sympathetic white students crowded into lunch counters across the city. The action was compared to the Boston Tea

Party that helped start the American Revolution. "The Greensboro Coffee Party" lasted six months and ended in victory. Woolworth desegregated its diners. At last, Joseph McNeil was able to sit down at the counter and eat a slice of apple pie.

Greensboro was one of the first cities where sit-ins took place. But it wasn't the last. Young people around the country decided to have sit-ins  in their own towns. One of those people was a college student in Nashville, Tennessee. His name was John Lewis. Along with fellow student Diane Nash and activist James Lawson, he helped form the Nashville Student Movement.

John Lewis

On February 13, 1960, John and the others led hundreds of Black and white students in sit-ins around Nashville. They were refused service at every lunch counter. White managers turned off the lights and closed the diners around them. The students sat in the dark until the end of the day.

After a few days of sit-ins, the police threatened to arrest the students. Angry white people beat and insulted them. Dr. King liked the young people's energy. He invited them to join his group—the Southern Christian Leadership Conference (SCLC). But the students thought the SCLC was too old-fashioned. Instead, they started their own group. It was called the Student Nonviolent Coordinating Committee, or SNCC, pronounced "snick" for short.

Student Nonviolent Coordinating Committee logo

SNCC came up with a plan they called "Jail, no bail." They got arrested and filled up the jails until the police couldn't arrest any more people.

Then SNCC marched to city hall. The mayor of Nashville was waiting on the steps. He was afraid the sit-ins would lead to violence.

Diane Nash asked him, "Do you recommend that lunch counters be desegregated?"

The mayor replied, "Yes."

SNCC had succeeded in just three months. The group was a new force in the civil rights movement. One that would play a big part in the future protests.

SNCC Rules of Nonviolence

Before the first sit-in, Lewis wrote up a list of nonviolent dos and don'ts to follow:

DO NOT

1. Strike back nor curse if abused.

2. Laugh out.

3. Hold conversations with floor walker.

4. Leave your seat until your leader has given you permission to do so.

5. Block entrances to stores outside nor the aisles inside.

DO

1. Show yourself friendly and courteous at all times.

2. Sit straight; always face the counter.

3. Report all serious incidents to your leader.

4. Refer information-seekers to your leader in a polite manner.

5. Remember the teachings of Jesus Christ, Mahatma Gandhi, and Martin Luther King. Love and nonviolence is the way.

MAY GOD BLESS EACH OF YOU

CHAPTER 5
Freedom Riders

On May 4, 1961, a group of Black and white students boarded buses for a new kind of protest called "Freedom Rides." The rides were organized by the Congress of Racial Equality (CORE). There had been many complaints from Black people who'd been blocked from using the bathrooms at bus stations across the South. The law said restrooms on national highways were for everyone. CORE teamed up with SNCC and SCLC. They planned to ride two buses from Washington, DC, to New Orleans, Louisiana, to draw attention to the problem.

John Lewis of SNCC was one of the thirteen original Freedom Riders. In South Carolina, he got off the bus and attempted to enter the white waiting room. A group of white youths in leather jackets blocked his way. After he told them it was against the law to stop him, they beat him up. Only after John was on his knees did the police tell the white men to go home.

John got back on the bus and kept riding. The farther south the two buses went, the more dangerous it became. In Alabama, the police allowed a mob to attack the buses. One bus was set on fire! The riders escaped and went to the

hospital, but the mob tried to burn it down, too. The bus drivers refused to go any farther. The first Freedom Ride was over, but there were more to come.

On May 17, a group of ten Freedom Riders rode south on a bus escorted by state police. They made it to Montgomery, Alabama, where the local police were supposed to protect them. Instead, the riders were attacked by a violent mob. Even then,

the riders would not turn around. As one white
Freedom Rider remembered, "The Black guys
and girls were singing. . . . They were so spirited
and so unafraid. They were really prepared to risk
their lives."

Freedom Songs

Singing played a big part in the civil rights movement. Traditional Black spirituals and hymns sung by protesters were known as freedom songs. One song became the anthem of the movement. "We Shall Overcome" started as a work song used by enslaved people in the South. They would work the fields while singing, "I'll be all right someday." In 1901, a minister changed the words to "I'll overcome someday."

Zilphia Horton

In 1945, striking South Carolina tobacco workers turned the word into "We will overcome." Two of those workers introduced it to activists and musicians including Zilphia Horton and Pete Seeger. They changed the lyrics to the way the song is sung today.

"I sang it with many different nationality groups. And it's so simple, and the idea's so sincere," Horton said.

They continued on to Mississippi. Mississippi was the most dangerous state in the South for civil rights protesters. There, they were arrested for disturbing the peace. They sang freedom songs and refused to eat. The riders stayed in jail for several weeks, but the protests continued. Over the next seven months, more than four hundred Freedom Riders rode buses south. In the end, the US government agreed to enforce the law. "Whites Only" signs came down at interstate rest stops and bus stations across the South. Once again, nonviolent protest had made a difference.

CHAPTER 6
The Children's Crusade

"Bombingham" was the terrible nickname for Birmingham, Alabama. The Klan regularly bombed the homes and churches of Black citizens there. Dr. King would later call it the most segregated city in the United States. But that did not stop Black people from demanding their civil rights. On the morning of May 2, 1963, thousands of children ages six to eighteen marched from the Sixteenth Street Baptist Church into downtown Birmingham. They wanted to end segregation—not just in Birmingham, but across

the nation. They called the march the Children's Crusade. A crusade is a fight for a cause that people believe in.

"I was told not to participate," Jessie Shepherd recalled. "But I was tired of the injustice." She was sixteen at the time. Many parents were afraid for

their children's safety. The city's commissioner for public safety was a white man named Bull Connor. At earlier civil rights protests in Birmingham, he'd had the police turn powerful fire hoses and brutal police dogs on marchers. But all of those

Bull Connor

protesters had been grown-ups. Dr. King and other civil rights leaders believed not even Connor would harm kids.

But they were wrong.

On the first day of the march, more than a thousand children were arrested. The youngest of them was only nine years old. They were jailed for as long as a week, or more. But the next day, more students marched. They carried protest signs and sang freedom songs. Less than two blocks from the church, Bull Connor's men were waiting. Out came the fire hoses.

Sixteen-year-old Arnetta Streeter recalled that she had clung to a friend and "the water just washed the two of us down the street." But she was one of the lucky ones. "I don't think I will ever forget that water, and when you would run they had the dogs waiting. I thank the lord that they didn't put the dogs on me," she said fifty years later.

Other children were bitten, beaten, and bruised. Some parents fought back to protect them. The news cameras caught it all for viewers at home. People sent bail money to free the kids from jail. The White House urged the city of Birmingham to negotiate with Dr. King.

In the end, Birmingham agreed to desegregate public areas. Black people could now also work in downtown stores. Dr. King called it "the most magnificent victory for justice we've seen in the Deep South."

The Klan held its own protest. A mass rally of Klansmen gathered in white hoods and robes. They burned large wooden crosses and threatened to kill Dr. King. They bombed his brother's house and the hotel where SCLC organizers and reporters often stayed. Violence broke out across the city. President Kennedy sent federal troops to keep the peace. But Dr. King told him more had to be done for civil rights.

Live on TV

The civil rights movement grew because of television. In 1957, two-thirds of all homes in the United States had a TV set. When the Little Rock Nine walked into school that first day, TV viewers were watching. They could hear the shouted insults. They could see the hatred and violence. For the first time, many white Americans saw what life was like for Black people.

The leaders of the civil rights movement immediately understood the power of television. In fact, they began to plan on it. As Dr. King later said, "We are here to say to the white men that we no longer will let them use clubs on us in the dark corners. We're going to make them do it in the glaring light of television." That "glaring light" shocked many Americans. It also convinced many of them to join the push for equality.

On June 11, 1963, President Kennedy spoke on television to the American people. He said, "This nation, for all its hopes and all its boasts, will not be fully free until all its citizens are free." He asked Congress to outlaw discrimination nationwide. But change was still slow to come.

John F. Kennedy

CHAPTER 7
The March on Washington

By 1963, there was a clear divide in the civil rights movement. One side moved carefully while the other wanted immediate change. A political group called the Nation of Islam supported the idea of Black Nationalism. That meant creating a separate country for Black people inside the United States. One of the leaders of the movement was a man who was named Malcolm X. He had been born Malcolm Little. *Little* was the name given to his enslaved ancestors by white men. He changed his last name to *X* to protest against slavery.

Malcolm X

Eventually, Malcolm X stopped believing in Black Nationalism. He began practicing the Islamic religion. He changed his name to el-Hajj Malik el-Shabazz and began to favor more peaceful methods for gaining equality. Unfortunately, the Nation of Islam did not agree with his new ideas. He was killed by members of that group in 1965.

Malcolm X once famously said, "We want freedom by any means necessary." This idea

went against the nonviolent practices of Dr. King and groups like SNCC. Several civil rights groups joined together for a big protest to prove nonviolence worked. They would go to the nation's capital, Washington, DC, and demand equality. They called it the March on Washington for Jobs and Freedom.

Organizers were determined to hold a peaceful event with both Black and white marchers. This meant getting permits, buses, food, and bathrooms for one hundred thousand people! The march started at the Washington Monument and ended at the Lincoln Memorial. (Abraham Lincoln was the president who ended slavery.) There would be music from famous singers, and the leaders of the civil rights movement would speak on the memorial steps.

Abraham Lincoln

On August 28, trains, buses, and carpools arrived from all across the country. One person traveled almost seven hundred miles to the march on roller skates! The crowd swelled to 250,000 marchers—more than twice the expected number! It was a hot day. People dangled their feet in the

pool between the two memorials. They sang songs and listened to speeches. Near the end of the day, Dr. King spoke some of the most famous words ever heard. His "I Have a Dream" speech was carried to the listeners at the march, and to TVs and radios around the world.

"I have a dream," he said, "that my four little children will one day live in a nation where they will not be judged by the color of their skin, but by the content of their character." He shared his belief that freedom would ring across the nation. All Americans would stand hand in hand and shout, "Free at last!"

The March on Washington was a great success. But for white supremacists, it was cause for violence. In "Bombingham," that meant the deaths of four innocent children.

Sixteenth Street Baptist Church

On a peaceful Sunday morning at the all-Black Sixteenth Street Baptist Church, four girls were in the basement getting ready for choir practice.

"I heard something that sounded, at first, a little like thunder and then just this terrific noise and the windows came crashing in," one churchgoer later recalled.

But it wasn't thunder. It was a bomb.

The four choir girls were killed instantly by the blast. Addie Mae Collins, Carole Robertson, and Cynthia Wesley were fourteen years old. Denise McNair was eleven.

Going clockwise: Addie Mae Collins, Cynthia Wesley, Carole Robertson, and Denise McNair

President Johnson signs the Civil Rights Act of 1964.

People took to the streets to protest their deaths. Support for the civil rights movement grew. The time for change had come, but the South would not budge. Lawmakers fought for five long months. At last, more than a year after President Kennedy had called for an end to discrimination, the Civil Rights Act of 1964 became law. It said the country would no longer allow discrimination on the basis of race, sex, religion, color, or national origin.

CHAPTER 8
Freedom Summer

For laws to work, people must obey them. For laws to be fair, people must be allowed to vote. But white Southerners continued to block Black voters' rights. This was especially true in Mississippi.

An American citizen must sign up in order to vote. There are offices to do this all over the 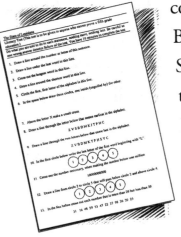 country. It should be easy. But for Black people in the South, it wasn't. When they tried to register in Mississippi, they were given difficult tests about US history—tests that white people didn't have to take. If Black people didn't pass the test, they couldn't vote. Sometimes, they were even failed for their handwriting!

Some voting offices were open only a few hours a day. They would keep changing their hours to make it harder to register. Black people would walk a long way only to find the office closed.

Some people were charged a voting tax they could not afford to pay. Those who did manage to register found their jobs and lives threatened if they tried to vote. So they did not try. As a result, they were not represented in local government. The laws that favored white people and harmed Black people remained unchanged.

In 1964, Black civil rights leaders decided to tackle the problem head-on. The Council of Federated Organizations (COFO) would recruit

Black and white student volunteers from around the country. These volunteers would travel to Mississippi to create Freedom Schools. The schools would educate Black people about their history and their civil rights. The volunteers would also help people register to vote. The project was called Freedom Summer.

Hundreds of students signed up. They met on a college campus in Ohio to train in nonviolence and safety. They were told to dress well and to drive below the speed limit to avoid trouble with the local police. But trouble was waiting.

On June 20, the first volunteers headed to Mississippi. Three of them went missing. Andrew Goodman and Michael "Mickey" Schwerner were both white men from New York. James Chaney was a young Black man from Mississippi. He had also been a Freedom Rider.

After a tense search that lasted nearly two months, all three men were found dead. They had been killed by Klansmen working with the local police.

Their deaths did not end Freedom Summer. Students of both races walked miles, stopping at houses and shacks to speak to poor people about their rights. They joined with local churches to sing freedom songs. For the first time in their lives, local Black people ate meals with white people. They opened their homes to the volunteers and learned that life could be different.

By the end of summer, Freedom Schools had taught over 2,500 children and adults. Seventeen thousand Black people had attempted to register to vote, even though many did not succeed. The volunteers also helped form a new group called the Mississippi Freedom Democratic Party, or MFDP.

Nearly half of the people in Mississippi were Black, but only white people held government offices. The MFDP fought to bring equal representation to Mississippi. Still, it took new laws and four more years before the majority of the state's Black voters were fully counted.

Mississippi Freedom Democratic Party

CHAPTER 9
Selma to Montgomery

Alabama was not much better than Mississippi when it came to letting Black people vote. The SCLC and SNCC decided to lead a series of protest marches in Selma, Alabama. They would ask TV news stations to cover the march. Any violence caught on camera might gain support for voters' rights.

On January 18, 1965, Dr. King and John Lewis began leading marches to the Selma courthouse. After a week of protests, the local sheriff beat a Black woman in full view of the cameras. Dr. King was arrested for having led the protest. In a letter published in the *New York Times* newspaper he said, "There are more Negroes in jail with me than there are on the voting rolls."

Nearly three weeks later, a civil rights activist named Jimmie Lee Jackson was shot and killed by state police. He'd been trying to stop them from beating his mother. To honor Jackson's life, the demonstrators planned a fifty-four-mile march from Selma to the steps of the state capitol building in Montgomery. The walk would take five days and risk lives. It was a chance most protesters were willing to take.

Jimmie Lee Jackson

On Sunday, March 7, John Lewis and members of the SCLC led over five hundred people in a peaceful march from Brown Chapel in Selma to the Edmund Pettus Bridge. They crossed the muddy waters of the Alabama River to face a terrifying sight. White policemen in helmets and blue uniforms stood waiting on the other side with nightsticks. They had been sent by Alabama's governor, George Wallace. Alabama State Police Major John Cloud shouted at the protesters through a bullhorn, "You will not be allowed to march any further!"

The protesters stood their ground and the police attacked. John Lewis's skull was fractured. Five women were beaten unconscious. Marchers hid under cars or scrambled down the riverbank. They were chased all the way back to Brown Chapel. The day became known as "Bloody Sunday." The violence shocked the world.

On March 21, over three thousand Black and white protesters set out once again. They included children, and the grandfather of Jimmie Lee Jackson. One white protester named Jim Letherer had only one leg. He planned to walk all fifty-four miles on crutches.

With news cameras rolling, the protesters

crossed the bridge. Angry white people lined the path of the march like it was a parade. They shouted insults and held signs telling the marchers to go home. But the protest went on. The marchers walked up to sixteen miles a day. Along the way, they were joined by celebrities and other supporters. Their numbers eventually

grew to twenty-five thousand people. On the last night of the march, they held a concert. The next morning, the marchers reached the steps of the state capitol. They demanded their voting rights. But Governor Wallace refused to see them. Still, the march was a success. The world had been watching. President Lyndon B. Johnson knew the time had come to show that he was on the side of civil rights.

John Lewis and Dr. King were there when the president signed the Voting Rights Act of 1965 into law. The new act made it illegal to give voters literacy tests. The federal government would investigate poll taxes and pay special attention to areas where hardly any voters were people of color. Black voices would no longer be ignored thanks to the Selma to Montgomery March. The promises first made by the Civil Rights Act of 1870 had finally been kept.

Lyndon B. Johnson signing the Voting Rights Act

CHAPTER 10
Changing Times

"Black Power!" became a rallying cry for some civil rights activists in the 1960s. A

man named Stokely Carmichael made the phrase popular. He described it as "a call for Black people in this country to unite, to recognize their heritage, to build a sense of community."

Stokely Carmichael

Black Power focused on people having pride in their African heritage. Natural hair and African-style clothing became fashionable. But like Black Nationalism, Black

Power encouraged Black people to live separately from white people.

In 1966, Black Power gave rise to the Black Panther Party in Oakland, California. The Black Panthers took their name from a group in Alabama whose goal was to get Black people elected into office. They'd chosen a black panther for their logo because it was the opposite of the white rooster logo used by the all-white Alabama Democratic Party.

The Black Panthers originally began in order to protect Black people from police brutality. The Panthers also offered free breakfasts to children, as well as health and education services to Black communities across the country. But the Black Panthers were different from other civil rights groups. They carried guns for protection and had trouble with the FBI. They did not agree with the nonviolent teachings of Dr. King.

Black Panther Party founders Bobby Seale (left) and Huey Newton

Much of the civil rights movement had been focused on the South. Discrimination in the rest of the country often went unnoticed until poor neighborhoods erupted in violence. This was the case in a Black neighborhood called Watts in Los Angeles, California. August 1965 marked six days of violence known as the Watts Riots. Violence also broke out in Northern cities like Chicago, New York, and Detroit.

Dr. King and the SCLC organized more peaceful protests, but none truly succeeded. In 1966, they launched the Chicago Freedom Movement, which worked with Operation Breadbasket to feed the poor. But discrimination in the North could be as difficult to overcome as it was in the South.

That same year, James Meredith attempted a "March Against Fear." Meredith was the man who had desegregated Ole Miss. Just two days into the walk, he was shot and wounded by a white man.

James Meredith is wounded during his "March Against Fear."

Organizers were determined to continue the march. But people like Stokely Carmichael were tired of the nonviolent approach. Carmichael called out "Black Power!" during the protest. The civil rights movement was becoming more extreme—and more divided.

Then, in April 1968, an event shook the entire country. Dr. King had gone to Memphis, Tennessee, in support of garbage collectors who demanded safer working conditions. On April 3, Dr. King gave a moving speech. He talked about his own death. There had been threats on his life, but he had always ignored them. In this speech he said that God had allowed him to go to the mountaintop and see the Promised Land. *The Promised Land* meant a peaceful world of Black and white people living together. "I may not get there with you," he told the crowd. "But I want you to know tonight that we, as a people, will get to the Promised Land."

The next evening, Dr. King was shot and killed on the balcony of his hotel. The assassin was a white man named James Earl Ray. Riots broke out across the country. The dream Dr. King had lived and died for was in danger of falling apart. And there was still a long way to go.

Unfortunately, progress is not always fast or easy. In 2008, Barack Obama became the first African American president of the United States. This was something that many Americans had hoped for but few believed they would live to see. The 2008 election seemed to promise the dawn of a new age of equality. Indeed, there are now more people of color in government and running major companies than ever before.

Inauguration of Barack Obama in 2009

Some people thought this meant racism no longer existed. But it does.

In the United States, people of color are still punished more severely by the law than white people. They are given much longer jail sentences for the same kinds of offenses. And Black people are still paid less for the same work.

In 2013, the Supreme Court overturned

part of the 1965 Voting Rights Act. Some Southern states immediately changed their laws to make it harder for people of color to vote. And white supremacy—the belief that white people are better than any other race—is on the rise. In Charlottesville, Virginia, in 2017, white supremacists marched while carrying torches and rifles, and shouting racist slogans.

But peaceful marches also continue. When a Black man named George Floyd was killed by police in 2020, the world rose up against it. Black Lives Matter marches were held worldwide to protest police brutality and the killing of African American men, women, and children. Many other minority groups still march to have their voices heard.

As Coretta Scott King, Dr. King's wife, said, "Freedom is never really won. You earn it and win it in every generation." And so the people march on.

Timeline of the Civil Rights Movement

1866 — The first Civil Rights Act becomes law

1896 — *Plessy v. Ferguson* introduces "separate but equal"

1909 — The NAACP forms

1942 — CORE, the Congress of Racial Equality, forms

1954 — *Brown v. Board of Education* declares "separate but equal" illegal

1955 — Emmett Till murdered

— Rosa Parks's arrest triggers Montgomery Bus Boycott

1957 — Little Rock Nine desegregate schools in Little Rock, Arkansas

1960 — Sit-ins begin in Greensboro, North Carolina

1961 — Freedom Rides begin

1963 — Martin Luther King Jr.'s "I Have a Dream" speech delivered at the March on Washington

1964 — Freedom Summer begins

— The Civil Rights Act of 1964 becomes law

1965 — Selma to Montgomery March

— Malcolm X is assassinated

1966 — Black Panther Party forms

1968 — Martin Luther King Jr. is assassinated

1986 — Martin Luther King Jr. Day becomes a national holiday

Timeline of the World

1860	Abraham Lincoln is elected president of the United States
1861	The Civil War begins, ending in 1865
1865	President Lincoln is killed by John Wilkes Booth
1886	The Statue of Liberty is given to the United States as a gift from the people of France for ending slavery
1906	An earthquake devastates San Francisco
1914	World War I begins, ending in 1918
1920	Women get the right to vote in the United States
1929	The Great Depression begins
1941	The United States enters World War II
1947	Jackie Robinson joins the Brooklyn Dodgers, intergrating modern major league baseball
1957	The Soviet Union launches Sputnik
1964	"Beatlemania" hits the United States
1967	Thurgood Marshall becomes the first Black US Supreme Court justice
1968	Franklin becomes the first African American character to appear in the comic strip *Peanuts*
1969	Neil Armstrong becomes the first person to walk on the moon
1977	*Star Wars* opens in theaters
1986	*The Oprah Winfrey Show* airs for the first time

Bibliography

*Books for young readers

*Curtis, Christopher Paul. *The Watsons Go to Birmingham—1963.* New York: Delacorte Books for Young Readers, 1995.

Davis, Townsend. *Weary Feet, Rested Souls: A Guided History of the Civil Rights Movement.* New York: W.W. Norton & Co., 1998.

Dierenfield, Bruce J. *The Civil Rights Movement (Revised Edition).* Harlow, England: Pearson Education Ltd., 2008.

*Fradin, Judith Bloom, and Dennis Brindell Fradin. *The Power of One: Daisy Bates and the Little Rock Nine.* New York: Clarion Books, 2004.

*Hoose, Phillip. *Claudette Colvin: Twice Toward Justice.* New York: Farrar, Straus and Giroux, 2009.

*Levinson, Cynthia. *We've Got a Job: The 1963 Birmingham Children's March.* Atlanta: Peachtree Publishing Company, 2012.

*Lewis, John, Andrew Aydin, and Nate Powell. *March, Books 1–3.* Marietta, GA: Top Shelf Productions, 2013–16.

Lewis, John, with Michael D'Orso. *Walking With the Wind: A Memoir of the Movement.* New York: Simon & Schuster, 1998.

Robinson, Jo Ann Gibson. *The Montgomery Bus Boycott and the Women Who Started It.* Knoxville: The University of Tennessee Press, 1987.

*Rubin, Susan Goldman. *Freedom Summer: The 1964 Struggle for Civil Rights in Mississippi.* New York: Holiday House, 2014.

*Taylor, Mildred D. *Roll of Thunder, Hear My Cry.* New York: Dial Press, 1976.

Linda Brown (left) with her family, Topeka, Kansas, 1954

People protesting integration of schools, 1956

Segregated bus station in Alabama, 1956

Rosa Parks being fingerprinted, 1956

Little Rock Nine students with National Guard,
Little Rock, Arkansas, 1957

Ruby Bridges is escorted into newly integrated school
by US Federal Marshals, 1960.

Sit-in protest at F.W. Woolworth Co., Greensboro, North Carolina, 1960

Freedom Riders bus is set on fire, 1961.

Wreckage from the church bombing that killed four girls,
Birmingham, Alabama, 1963

March on Washington for Jobs and Freedom, August 28, 1963

Massive crowd at the March on Washington for Jobs and Freedom,
August 28, 1963

Civil rights leader John Lewis, 1964

Civil rights demonstrators during Freedom Summer, 1964

Martin Luther King Jr. leading the march from
Selma to Montgomery, Alabama, March 1965

Marchers cross the Edmund Pettus Bridge, Selma, Alabama, March 1965.

Black activist Stokely Carmichael, 1967

Assassination of Martin Luther King Jr., 1968

President Lyndon B. Johnson signing Civil Rights Act of 1968

Black Panther Party members, 1968

Barack Obama sworn in as the forty-fourth US president, 2009

Black Lives Matter march, July 2020